Stone image. (Bishop Museum)

He Ola Ka Pohaku . . .
There is Life in the Stone and Death in the Stone . . .

—Ancient Hawaiian Saying

A few years ago a Hawaiian family living on the windward side of Oahu sold their family home and bought a new condominium in Honolulu. Two days before they were to leave, the father began calling friends, asking, "Do you want some *pohaku*s?" He was looking for someone to take the *imu* stones that, as a child, he had helped his father and uncle move there from his grandfather's home. Late the next day, as it was beginning to get dark, the man's last act in his old home was to gather up the old *imu* stones and load them in a pickup to be hauled to a new home across the island.

The man may not have thought out all the reasons why he wanted the stones to go to someone who would appreciate them, but he was acting in a manner his ancestors would have understood. To them, stones, like all things in the universe, had an element of being—of power and life beyond the obvious. Some stones were inhabited by spirits, some had *mana* or spiritual power, and others were just nice to have around.

1

According to tradition, some spirits became part of a rock and never left it. Stories about how they got there were forgotten. Other spirits used stones as a home or a place to stay only part of the time. Some entered their stones by their own choice, while others became part of a stone when, as a person, they were turned into a rock by a supernatural being.* Some, through the spirits in them, acted as guardians of various places. Others had the power to bestow health and to assure growth or fertility. Certain stones were used by *kahunas* for divination, while others provided a place for humans to leap into the next life.

All these stones had personal names and many are still known today. The *pohaku wa'uwa'u'ili* was found offshore at Waikupuna, Kau, on the island of Hawaii. Called "stone that claws the skin," it was believed that if a person could entice a would-be lover to this stone and scratch his or her skin a strong attachment would result.

Thin, "the flatter the better," water-polished, black stones were sometimes put under a person's pillow to keep their spirit from wandering. Similar stones were used by some families to attract positive forces into their home. These stones generally were given names with family meanings.

All kinds of stones—fine-grained stones, porous stones, lava stones, coral stones—were used to build *heiaus*, shrines, fish ponds, house foundations, and taro-patch walls. Each stone was chosen for its appropriate size, shape, and similarity to the other stones being used. This contributed to the *mana* of the structure. Structures received further *mana* through prayers and offerings, or from the personal *mana* of the people who used them. These structures also had personal names.

David Malo, one of the first Hawaiian writers, wrote an essay on stones in which he classified them according to their size: "The ancients called rocks *pohaku*. A rocky cliff was called *pali pohaku* or cliff stone. Smaller stones were called *pohaku uuku iho*. Still smaller stones were *'a'a*. Still smaller yet were *'ili'ili* or pebbles. Very small stones

---

* Stories of people being turned into stones may be a symbolic way of saying they were killed.

Old stone wall in the Hawaiian style, Kalawao, Molokai. (Judi Thompson)

Sacrificial stone, Hilo Heiau. (T. Kelsey, Bishop Museum)

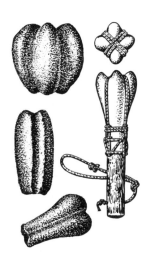

Relief carving on a stone found in Moanalua. (Bishop Museum)

Hawaiian quoits: small, flat, rounded pieces of stone used in a pitching game. (Bishop Museum)

War clubs made of carefully shaped stones lashed to wooden handles. (From Joseph Feher's *Hawaii: A Pictorial History*. Reprinted courtesy of Bishop Museum.)

Lava rock poi-pounder with gourd. (Larry Lau, BYU—HC Archives)

Old Hawaiian smoother found on Molokai. (Richard Marks Collection)

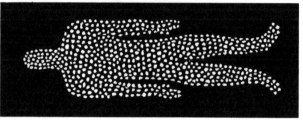

Sling *(ma'a)* and stones, a weapon of war in Hawaii. (Bishop Museum)

Figure formed of pebbles served apprentice *kahuna*s as a device for learning the symptoms of various illnesses. (From Joseph Feher's *Hawaii: A Pictorial History*. Reprinted courtesy of Bishop Museum.)

Stone lamps, used for burning *kukui*-nut oil or strings of *kukui* nuts to light Hawaiian homes. (From Joseph Feher's *Hawaii: A Pictorial History*. Reprinted courtesy of Bishop Museum.)

were sand or *one*. The very finest was *lepo* or dirt."* Malo went on to list the types of stones used in making adzes, squid-fishing hooks, *maika* game stones, canoe-smoothing and polishing stones, and *poi* pounders. In all, he named fifty-eight different types of stones. These stories are about the names, lives, personalities, histories, and uses of stones in Hawaii.

1

The Stones of Umi

Around 1500 Umi a Liloa became the ruling chief of the island of Hawaii. According to tradition, sometime after that he decided to take a census of the people, and he announced that the count would be made by stones. Each person living on the island was to bring a stone to a designated spot, its size determined by the age and strength of the person to carry it.

Umi chose Kaili Heiau, high up on the side of the volcanic mountain Hualalai, about twenty miles above Kealakekua, as the place for the counting. Although today that location seems out of the way, there is evidence that at least one good roadway existed there in ancient times. It ran from the Kau district to Kailua-Kona.

When preparations were completed, the people began to come from all parts of the island. At the direction of the guards, each person placed a stone on the pile representing their district. There were eight piles of stones outside the *heiau*. Some say each of the piles, resembling pyramids, pointed to the district of its builders. The pile for Kona was the largest, and the one for Kohala was next in size. Some of the piles are said to have been over twenty-five feet across and at least fifteen feet high. Today many of these same stones remain, as do fragments of the *heiau* walls, which at their base were once seven feet thick.

---

* Translated from Hawaiian by Theodore Kelsey, from a holographed copy made circa 1870 of David Malo's "Hawaiian Antiquities."

Some old-timers say that this form of census-taking gave the mountain its name, Hualalai. Tradition has it that *hu* means to rise, *ala* signifies the stones brought by the people for the census, and *lai* refers to the spread of the pile.

It is uncertain why Umi chose this location for his census. According to one story, the reason goes back to the time when Keliiokaloa was high chief in the Kona district, and the first white people, a man and a woman, landed in Hawaii. These two, believed to have been a brother and sister, apparently escaped from a ship that was wrecked off Kealakekua. In time each took a Hawaiian mate, and the foreign pair's descendants became part of the chiefly line that produced Liliha and her daughter Loheau. All the other districts of the island were under the control of Umi. Keliiokaloa was Umi's political enemy and a cruel and destructive chief. Sometime after the foreigners' arrival, Umi declared war on Keliiokaloa.

The two armies met on the elevated plain on the side of Hualalai. The fighting was bloody, but in the end Umi was the victor, becoming sole ruler of the island. One version of the story says that the Ahua a Umi was built to commemorate that battle. It also says that the people of the six provinces built six of the pyramid-shaped piles of lava rock collected in the neighborhood. Umi's chiefs and warriors built a seventh stone pile. Some speculate that Umi may have been buried in the eighth pile.

In the center of these large, pyramid-shaped rock structures Umi built a *heiau*. He also built one at the foot of Pohaku Hanalei on the Kona coast, called Ahua Hanalei; another one on the slopes of Mauna Kea "in the direction of Hilo," at a place called Puu Keekee; and a fourth one on Mauna Halepohaha.

It is interesting to note that these *heiau*s built by Umi all have four more or less equal-sized square compartments divided by cross-shaped interwalls. One compartment is said to be dedicated to the god Kaili, one to Ku, and one to Lono. The fourth is called the Place of Umi. Some speculate that Umi may have been inspired by the Christian cross of the two foreigners because that style of division within a *heiau* is rare. Others believe that the site was chosen for astrological observations and was aligned to certain stellar phenomena.

This story is based on material given by Elizabeth Pestana; an anonymous informant; Albert S. Baker, "Ahua a Umi," Thrum's *Hawaiian Annual* (1917); and Jules Remy, *Contributions of a Venerable Savage to the Ancient History of the Hawaiian Islands,* 1868.

2
The Healing Stones of Wahiawa

On a side street in Wahiawa are two stones said to have healing powers. One is shaped like a shoe, and the other has been compared to a surfboard or a tongue. The surfboard-shaped stone is about six feet tall and just over two feet wide. Today some Hawaiians say the name of that stone is Pohaku Ho'ola Kino, or "Rock that gives health to the body." Older sources give the name as Kaniniulaokalani. No one seems to know the name of the shoe-shaped rock.

Some stories about these stones conflict. One story says that the stones are two sisters who were turned into rocks many generations ago. According to that account the sisters lived on Kauai. For some reason they decided to visit Kukaniloko, Oahu's famous birthplace of chiefs, and flew there using supernatural powers. However, their powers were effective only during hours of darkness. Only a short distance from Kukaniloko they were struck by the first rays of the sun. Turned into stones, they fell along the bank of the stream in Kaukonahua gulch.

The two stones stayed along the stream bank until some time in the early 1900s when the road through Kaukonahua was being widened. During construction a large stone was dislodged and thrown to the side of the road. That night the *haole* supervisor, George Galbraith, had a dream about the stone. According to his own account, he heard a voice that kept repeating, "You have my feet up and my head

Dedication at Kukaniloko by the Daughters of Hawaii, 1925. (Ken Coffey)

down, please turn me around." When he awakened he recognized the stone in his dream as the one he had moved to the side of the road. Haunted by the dream, Galbraith had his workmen turn the stone over. Two old Hawaiian men who helped turn over the stone told the supervisor that the name of the stone was Kaniniulaokalani and that it held a legendary spirit that should be cared for. Out of respect for the old men's belief, Galbraith had a bullock cart move the stone to the clearing at Kukaniloko Heiau.

Whatever the truth of their ancient history, the two rocks were at Kukaniloko in 1925 when the Daughters of Hawaii rededicated the *heiau* there. According to several versions of the story, leis were ceremonially placed on each of the birth stones, and someone impulsively put leis on the two stones that had been moved there during the road building.

About the same time, workers from the pineapple fields surrounding the *heiau* began to visit the spot and were soon reporting miraculous cures. As the stories spread, crowds flocked to the spot. People would pray there, leave offerings, and sometimes burn fires in front of the tall stone. Some even left money on the ground. No one seemed to know why the tall stone received such special attention.

Unable to maintain the popular site, the Daughters of Hawaii decided to have the stones moved. According to one story, the workmen began to move the tall stone but it crumbled into pieces. Some thought it a sign that the stone did not want to be moved to an out-of-the-way place. After being put back together with cement, it was moved to the Wahiawa cemetery. The smaller stone was also moved, although no reason was given. The fact that the two stones were not simply pushed back into the gulch argues for their traditional importance.

After the stones were moved to Wahiawa, they became even more popular. There the smaller stone acquired the reputation of having special healing powers for women and young children. On a typical day, visitors began to arrive at dawn. Pineapple workers on their way to the fields would stop to say a prayer or leave an offering. A writer in 1929 described the scene:

> There are Chinese who drive inland from Honolulu, their women in gorgeous silk trousers; Hawaiians with hibiscus flowers tucked behind their ears; Korean women in bright green blouses with high-waisted full skirts; Filipino boys with wreaths of fresh roses round their hats; tiny Japanese ladies in Kimonos of rich colors, with porcelain-like coiffures adding charm to their exquisitely poised heads. . . .
>
> The eerie, exciting smell of incense hangs heavy in the air. Some kneel, at a distance from the enclosure, mumbling prayers aloud. Some are caressing the tall god, hanging leis around him, blessing jars of water, lighting fires and sweet-smelling punk. Others lean on the fence, staring at those two very plain-looking stones. . . .
>
> Nearby have been erected stalls for the sale of leis, bottles of water, incense, fruit and candies. The lei-sellers do not call to

Wahiawa healing stones at the height of their popularity during the 1920s. (Williams Studio photo, Hawaii State Archives)

people and beg them to buy as they do on the wharves; they sit with dignity and tell legends of the two gods. . . .

By mid-afternoon schoolchildren might join the crowd, either to pray for a personal or family need, or to satisfy their curiosity. Before the day was over, more workers might stop on their way home and often there were nighttime visitors. When all was quiet and the last visitor had left, there would likely be an array of food, candies, leis, Chinese prayer-papers, and an occasional crucifix before the stones. Apparently there was always money. It has been said that during 1927 as much as a thousand dollars a month was left. After a time, the local water company that owned the land decided to use the money to improve the road to the area and provide parking.

Skeptics who did not believe in the stones' powers were upset by such public acclaim and tried to keep people away. The Board of Health was called in because some feared an epidemic might break out. Several cultures were taken from the stones and analyzed. Despite negative results, the stones were disinfected twice a day and a strict schedule of cleaning the grounds was maintained.

With the outbreak of World War II and the accompanying gas shortage, curfews, and long working hours, the number of visitors to the stones decreased. A Japanese shrine-like crypt was erected over the stones in 1948 at the present location at 108 California Street in Wahiawa. The old Wahiawa cemetery is now covered by a housing development. Today only a few people visit the site.

This story is based on the personal notes of the late Lahilahi Webb; stories that appeared in the *Honolulu Star-Bulletin* during September 1936; Ruth McKelway, "The Stone Gods of Wahiawa," *Asia Magazine,* February 1929; Henry Lum and M. Miyazawa, "An Abortive Religious Cult," *Social Process* 7 (November 1941): 20–24; and the personal reminiscences of the late Ned Burgess as told to Kalahikiola Spotkaeff.

3
Season-measuring Stones

On the easternmost point of the island of Hawaii, in the Puna district, are a number of stones believed to have been used in ancient times to measure the divisions of the year. Both the point on which they stand and a pillar of stone on the northern border of the cape were named for Kumukahi, said to be the younger brother of the Polynesian adventurer Moikeha and a cousin of the volcano goddess, Pele.

Standing opposite the stone Kumukahi, on the same side of the point, was once a monolith called Makanoni. The name, which has been translated as "Speckled-face," was given in honor of one of Kumukahi's wives. In the summer, when the sun is at its northern point, it shone on Kumukahi, and in the season of cool weather the sun moved and passed over to Makanoni.

Another wife of Kumukahi was Kanono, whose name means "Very-red-sunburn." Her name and, some believe, her spirit were given to a rock in the sea. When the rising sun's light struck that rock, the people knew that the sun had reached its southern limit, and the days would become longer. That day is now called the first day of winter.

A large stone on land is said to have been still another wife of Kumukahi. It was called Paupoulu, or "Skirt-made-of-breadfruit-bark." When the light from the rising sun struck this stone it had reached its northern limit, and the days would begin to grow shorter. Now that day is called the first day of summer.

Two other stones in the area are also said to have been wives of Kumukahi: Hanakaulua, or "Take-plenty-of-time-to-work," and Haehae, whose name has been translated as "Rent-assunder." A stone named Haula or "Fall Leaves" may or may not have been a wife. Another stone, Kahinaakala, or "Sunrise," is believed to have been a sister. Some speculate that one of these stones might have been used to measure solstices and equinoxes.

Tradition has it that the area was a place of healing where the sick were brought for treatment. In addition to the special offerings made by the sick at Kumukahi, all sun worshippers came once a year to bring offerings.

It is interesting to note that the winds coming from the ocean divide at Kumukahi Point. One current of wind blows on Hilo, the other past Haula down the rugged Puna coast.

Material for this article came from notes shared by Mary Kawena Pukui; Abraham Fornander, *Hawaiian Antiquities* (1916–1917), vol. 4, pp. 156–160; N. B. Emerson, *Unwritten Literature of Hawaii* (1906), p. 197; Laura C. Green and Martha Warren Beckwith, "Hawaiian Customs and Beliefs Relating to Sickness and Death," *American Anthropologist* 28, no. 1 (1926): 176–208; C. B. Taylor, "Little Tales from Hawaii," *Honolulu Star-Bulletin,* February 3, 1960. Miss Taylor's informant on Kumukahi was Mary Kawena Pukui.

Wahinenui woke everyone
in the middle of the night.
(Ken Coffey)

4

Kaneikokala

In the half-light of Hawaii Hall at the Bernice P. Bishop Museum, between two display cases, is a rough-shaped stone with a slightly *kapakahi* (crooked) face. The stone is a god-figure from ancient times named Kaneikokala. A story tells how, like many other famous stones of Hawaii, it "chose" a *kahu* (caretaker).

An old man named Wahinenui and his son Hueu lived near a fish pond at Kawaihae on the island of Hawaii. A boy of about thirteen or fourteen, James Poai, and his sister, Sara, also lived with the old man. Sometime around 1885, according to James Poai, Wahinenui became "peculiar."

One night very late, Wahinenui woke everyone in the house. He was dressed in a *malo* (loincloth), a shirt, a necktie, and a Prince Albert coat and carried a long, sword-like knife by his side. He sent his son, Hueu, to get his fishnet and then told him to go to the fish pond to catch three mullet. James was sent to cut a bunch of coconuts from a tree and told to carry them down the tree on his back so that the nuts would not fall to the ground. Sara was told to chew one mouthful of *'awa* (Polynesian opiate plant).

When the fish, coconuts, and 'awa were ready, Wahinenui sent the children for picks and shovels. The four then went down the road about three hundred feet to the home of their neighbor, Lalapali. Lalapali had many dogs, but that night, strangely, not one of them barked.

At Lalapali's home Wahinenui marked a spot on the ground and told Hueu, James, and Sara to dig. They dug until they found water. When they stopped, the old man told them to keep digging until their picks hit something hard. They dug deeper and finally struck something. Not sure of what they had found, they tried to lift it out of the hole but could not. They then went to awaken the Lalapali family to ask for help.

What they had found was a large, rough-shaped stone. When it was out of the ground Wahinenui took the cup of 'awa and poured it by the stone's mouth as an offering. After that he took the three mullet and placed them in front of the stone. Then he took the bunch of coconuts and hung them around the stone's neck.

After the offerings were made, they carried the stone inside Lalapali's gate and left it there. Wahinenui told them that the stone's name was Kaneikokala. He also told them that he would die in three days' time. Three days later the old man died, exactly as he had predicted.

The stone, fifty-eight inches high, was given to the Bishop Museum in 1939. At the same time, this story about the stone was told to Lahilahi Webb by James Poai and is part of the Museum's records.

Pohaku Kaneikokala rests in Hawaii Hall at the Bishop Museum. (Ben Patnoi, Bishop Museum)

5

Birth Stones of Hawaii

In ancient times two places were famous as the birth sites of high-ranking children. They were Kukaniloko, Oahu (sometimes written Kukaniloku), and Wailua, Kauai. At both places there were great stones that supported chiefly mothers in a semi-sitting position while giving birth.

Kukaniloko is not far from Wahiawa on the plains of Halemano in the Waialua district. It is said that the *heiau* there was built for the birth of Kapawa, son of the chief Nanakaoko and his wife Kahihiokalani. The name Kukaniloko has been translated as "an inland area from which great events are heralded." According to tradition, "If anyone came in confident trust and lay properly upon the supports (stones) the child would be born with honor. It would be called a chief divine: a burning fire." If by some chance the mother-to-be did not make it to the *heiau* and the child was born outside, it would be called an *iwahu* (outside chief).

Kamehameha I had hoped that his children by his *kapu* wife, Keopuolani, would be born there, but at the time of the birth of each of her children something prevented her from traveling to Oahu.

When a child was to be born at Kukaniloko many people accompanied the expectant parents. It is said that a thousand *maka'ainana* (commoners) would be assembled on the east side of Kuakikua stream, which flows near the *heiau*, while personal servants of the chiefs waited on the south side of the stream. Facing the stone on which the mother-to-be would deliver were two rows of eighteen stones each. Tradition has it that the stones were inhabited by *'aumakua* (guardian spirits) who had the power to absorb pain. A chief stood in front of each stone.

When the child was born two large *kapu* drums named Hawea and Opuku were sounded to announce the birth. Then the child was quickly taken inside the *waihau* (inner temple) of Hoolonopahu where the drums were kept. There the ceremony of cutting the umbilical

16

cord was performed. Forty-eight chiefs took part in the accompanying rituals. The following chant honors the sacred site of Kukaniloko.

He Mele No Kukaniloko
A Song of Kukaniloko

No Kukaniloko ko'u aloha,
For Kukaniloko is my love,

Ke kupa noho kula a o Kalakoa,
The native born that dwells on the plain of Kalakoa

Kahi hanau hoi o na alii,
Birth place indeed of the chiefs

Wohi hoi a o Hawaii nei;
Highest chiefs indeed of Hawaii here

Walea i ke kui lei Ahihi,
Accustomed to stringing wreaths of *ahihi* [jasmine]

Lei hookipa no ka malihini;
Wreath of entertainment for the stranger

Paa mai uka i ka uhiwai,
Finished from upland in the heavy mist

O ke kehau anu ko ke kuahiwi;
The cold dew of the mountain

Halihali mai ana i ke ala,
Bearing the fragrance

Ke ala o maile Nohoanu;
The fragrance of *mana* that dwells in the cold

Auau aku i ka wai o Kuaikua
Bathe in the water of Kuaikua

Wai hooheno a na'lii;
Cherished water of the chiefs

Na mamo hoi a Kakuhihewa,
The descendants indeed of Kakuhihewa

A na pua a ka Na'i Aupuni;
The offspring of the Conqueror of the Realm

Nana i rula mai a pololei,
Who ruled wisely

Me ka ihe laumeki i ka lima;
With the barbed spear in the hand

A he puuwai koa me ka wiwoole;
And a brave heart with fearlessness

Imi maluhia no ka lahui;
Seeking peace for the race.

Hui pau ia mai na ailana,
All united are the islands

Mai Hawaii a Niihau,
From Hawaii to Niihau

Noho hoomalu ia me ke kaulike
Dwelling in peace with justice

Mamalahoa kanawai;
Mamala Hoa is the law

Hainaia mai ana ka puana,
Told is the refrain

No Kukaniloko ko'u aloha.
For Kukaniloko is my love.

Birth of an alii, Kukaniloko, Oahu. (Ken Coffey)

A second important birth site is located on the north side of the Wailua River at the base of Puuki Ridge on Kauai. The place is called Holoholoku. Only two stones remain of those that were once famous for giving *mana* (life force) to the child born there. An old saying gives some idea of the importance attached to this place:

The child of a chief born at Holoholoku becomes a high chief.
The child of a commoner born at Holoholoku becomes a chief, also;
The child of a high chief born outside of Holoholoku is no chief, a commoner he!

Other stones once well known as birth stones are the Naha Stone in Hilo and the Pohakuloa stone at the Wilder gate of Punahou School in Honolulu. The latter stone was originally at Round Top on Oahu and was moved with the permission of Kamehameha III. At one time a Japanese consul living at the corner of Beretania and Makiki Streets was given a part of the Punahou stone for his garden. Some years later the first maternity home in Hawaii was built on that site. Some believe that the *mana* of the stone brought about that choice.

Iolekaa in Haiku Valley is also said to have birth stones. Petroglyphs found there seem to indicate a birth scene.

The material for this story was taken from conversations with Sammy Amalu and Sam Lono; an article by Charles Kenn based on the recollections of William Malahea; and articles that appeared in *Ka Nupepa Kuokoa* and Thrum's *Hawaiian Annual*, 1912. The chant for Kukaniloko was composed by John Holani Hao and appeared in *Ka Nupepa Kuokoa* on May 25, 1925. It was translated by Theodore Kelsey.

Stones of Kukaniloko, Wahiawa, Oahu. (Daughters of Hawaii)

Birth stone located at the Wilder gate, Punahou School, Honolulu. (Judi Thompson)

Petroglyphs at a *heiau lapaau* depict a birth scene, Lanakila, Oahu. (Bud Henry)

6
Hupeloa, a Stone at Kolekole Pass

Some of the stories about Hawaiian stones are very old and have been told over and over with little change. Other stories have been forgotten, and still others are of recent creation. The stories about the stone Hupeloa which follow are no exception. Some are traditional. However, two stories came into being just sixty years ago.

Kolekole Pass is across the ridge of the Waianae mountain range that separates Leeward Oahu from the Wahiawa plateau. The road follows an ancient trail. At the top of the pass, just off the road, is the stone, Hupeloa. One of the stories about the stone says that *lua* (Hawaiian wrestler) fighters used the area to practice. Mary Kawena Pukui translates the name Kolekole as "to strip the flesh," a name most likely given to the pass because of the wounds received by the *lua* fighters.

Another story says that the site was used to prepare the bodies of chiefs for burial. There, according to Hawaiian custom, the bodies were placed in an *imu* (earth oven) to hasten the deterioration of the flesh, which was then stripped off *(kolekole)*. In this case the stone's name, Hupeloa, which can refer to deteriorating flesh, would be especially appropriate. After the bodies were prepared for burial they were taken to Nioula Heiau on Halona ridge in Lualualei. It is said to have been built by the ancient chief Kakuihewa and is a *heiau* of the *poo kanaka* (wise men) class.

Stories also tell of a spirit in the stone that guards the pass. People ascending the pass have a safe trip if they travel by day and leave an offering at the stone. Night travelers have no such guarantee.

One persistent story about Hupeloa says that the stone was used to drain blood from human sacrifices. But the story is not an authentic one for it began only about sixty years ago. The late Lahilahi Webb, who was associated with the Bernice P. Bishop Museum for many years and considered an authority on Hawaiiana, attributed the tale to her cousin, Mrs. Rose Murray White, who unintentionally started the story. At the pass one day a party of which Mrs. White was a member

Hupeloa today. (Judi Thompson)

came upon the stone and she was asked, " 'What kind of stone is this?' She replied that it looked something like a sacrificial rock. She pointed to the grooved sides and hollowed cup in the side where perhaps was collected the blood of animals sacrificed to the gods.'' Mrs. White's half-joking, casual comment became the basis of the rumor of animal blood sacrifices despite the fact that knowledgeable old Hawaiians and anthropologists hold firmly to the belief that although Hawaiians made both animal and human sacrifices, they never made blood sacrifices.

Another story about the stone began just before World War II when the military road over the pass was under construction. Reportedly, construction workers moved the stone to one side of the road because it was in the way. The next day the stone had returned to its original spot. Several times the stone was moved, but each time it moved back. Finally, the construction company decided to change the road a few feet and leave the stone ''where it wanted to be.''

The stories of Hupeloa come from Maryknoll Kalahikiola Spotkaeff; Jan Kahalewai Merriman; the notes of Mary Kawena Pukui; a column, "Schofield Snapshots," by V. H. Herald, dated September 1936, from an unidentified newspaper; Mary Kawena Pukui et al., *Place Names of Hawaii,* 1974; and Elspeth P. Sterling and Catherine C. Summers, *Sites of Oahu,* 1978 [1962].

7
'Ili'ili Hula-Dance Stones

In ancient times *hula* dancers frequently sought out water-washed stones along the seashore or in streambeds. They were looking for flat, thin stones about an inch and a half to two inches in diameter. Porous stones, frequently called female stones, were discarded in favor of fine-grained stones believed to be male.

These *'ili'ili* stones, sought even today by dancers, were used as musical instruments and were played in much the same manner as Spanish castanets. According to the late Iolani Luahine, the size and shape of the stones chosen depended on the person who would be using them. There is a difference in the tone and sound made by stones of various sizes and thicknesses. There is also a difference in the sound made by the clicking together of two female or two male stones.

If the stones were to be used for special purposes, such as dancing the sacred *hula*s or chiefly *inoa*s (name chants), the dancers would prepare themselves with prayers and offerings before going to collect their stones. If the stones were to be used for dances such as those performed at the hotels, the collecting would be more of a good-time excursion.

On each of the islands there were special places that dancers went to find the *'ili'ili* stones for dancing. Some of these were Ninole in Kau, Makapala, Kohala, Punaluu on the windward side of Oahu, Nuuanu stream, and Maili on the Waianae Coast. Unfortunately, many of these places have been lost to development.

Although the stones were to be had for the gathering, they required care once they were chosen. They were kept clean, rubbed with *kukui*-nut oil, wrapped in *tapa* or soft cloth, and stored where they could not be handled by anyone but the dancer. According to Miss Luahine, ''If you take care of what you have, what you have will take care of you.''

Stones were also important to some *halau hula* (hula academies) because they were believed to be resting places for the spirit of the *hula*

Elongated waterworn stones wrapped in tapa and leaves, often left as offerings at sacred sites. (Bishop Museum)

Punaluu beachfront, a favorite source of *'ili'ili* stones. (Judi Thompson)

god Laka. According to the late royal chanter, Kuluwaimaka, a black, smooth, water-washed *ala* stone was placed in a bower made of four branches of *'ohi'a*, tied tepee-like, at about eye level. Other *halau hula* used a block of *lama* wood for the spirit's resting place.

Material for this section came from oral interviews with the late Iolani Luahine, Kaupena Wong, and Mililani Allen, as well as from Theodore Kelsey, whose source was Kuluwaimaka, a chanter for both Queen Emma and King Kalakaua.

8
Ku'ula and *Koa,* the Stones of the Fishermen

Perhaps the most important stones in ancient times were the *ku'ula* and *koa* stones of the fishermen. *Koa* stones—either natural stone outcrops or stone piles used for marking and finding fishing grounds—could be located near fishing grounds or simply used to triangulate their location. Some *koa* were nothing more than piles of stones built up in the ocean by members of a fishing family. Such *koa* might be markers for a natural fishing ground or serve to attract a fish colony.

Ku'ula stones were believed to contain a spirit that attracted fish and helped fishermen. They could be either naturally shaped stones or slightly worked. According to tradition, the naturally shaped stones contained a spirit, either placed there by the gods or there of its own choice. A man-made *ku'ula* was believed to receive its spirit only after appropriate prayers and offerings had been made. The *ku'ula* could be either of black- or light-colored stone; some said that the dark stones were male and the light ones female.

A naturally formed *ku'ula* might be found by a fisherman realizing that the stone contained a spirit. Other times, it was believed, a stone chose a fisherman for its *kahu* (caretaker). It might come to him in a dream, saying, "I am cold, come and get me." The fisherman would ask, "What do you say? Where are you?" The stone would then describe just where it was and how to find it, what to bring as an offering,

"Akua" stones. (Bishop Museum)

and when to come for it. Sometimes the stone would not reveal what it wanted the first time it appeared in a dream. It might take days, weeks, or even months before the stone revealed its whereabouts. If the stone was female and the dreamer a man, the stone might even flirt with him.

The dreamer would search for the stone, carefully following all the directions given by the *ku'ula*. When found, the stone would have the mouth of a fish. It would then be taken home and put in a *kapu* (taboo) place where nothing could disturb it. Only the guardian chosen by the stone could handle it. It was believed that if others handled it and the stone did not wish them to, it would become hot like fire.

Those who had *ku'ula* stones believed that caring for them was as serious as caring for a baby. The guardian would ask the *pohaku* (stone) what it wanted. The answer would come in a dream or vision. The *ku'ula* had to be fed three meals a day. If even one meal were missed, the guardian could be in for trouble. It also needed clothing—a *malo* (loincloth) that could be wrapped around the stone or used as a blanket. The *malo* had to be kept very clean.

According to tradition, if the stone was well cared for and all of the requirements met, its guardian would profit richly. It was said that the more you gave the stone, the more fish you would catch. Lights, laughter, and activity would bless the home of the caretaker.

Sometimes the *ku'ula* would vanish. Like a little child it would go out to play and disappear. But apparently it always knew when it was time to come home and would then reappear.

A person in need of help would traditionally make offerings to the stone and wait. It might take days or even months, but when the stone was ready, it would give the location of a school of fish. It would also tell what time of day the fish would appear and what line or net and bait to use. When caught, the fish were to be shared with everyone. Pregnant women customarily received double the share of others.

A *ku'ula* could be used for generations. When the guardian had grown old, the stone would tell him who the next caretaker should be. It would know which child in the family should carry on the tradition. It was believed that the stone could "fall in love" with anyone.

Sometimes the *ku'ula* would be given to a member of the family, but the guardian would not tell the chosen person the purpose of the stone. One night the stone would come to its new caretaker and reveal its name, its work, and how to care for it. It could be within a few days or it might take years.

Belief in the *ku'ula* and *koa* stones continues. The traditions surrounding them are still practiced by some, and the recipient of such a stone must care for it. Its powers are unknown and untapped. The stone may be a source of power for good, and, if treated with respect, one that will reward its guardian richly.

The material for this article was collected over the years from George Ai, Louis Aila, Ned Burgess, Arthur K. Cathcart, Ah Sam Cheong, Thomas Maunupau, Kalahikiola Naluelua, Henry Young, and Maryknoll Kalahikiola Spotkaeff.

9
Pohaku Hanau, Stones That Give Birth

According to tradition, another group of stones holds particular importance for Hawaiians: stones that *hanau* (give birth) and the stones that are born to them. These stones, which are considered female, are porous, and a close look reveals small stones in the surface holes. The male stones in these families are smooth and close grained. It is said that if a person gathers both a male and a female stone and keeps them covered with water, "by and by the female pebbles give birth."

One place famous for *hanau* stones is Koloa, Punaluu, in the Kau district of the Big Island. The *hanau* stones found at Punaluu are generally small enough to be held in the palm of one hand. However, larger stones were also believed to give birth. Along the Hilo shoreline and along the Wailuku River are at least two of these stone "families." One is that of a chief of the Puueo area who mated with Namaka, a chiefly woman of Piihonua. Tradition has it that some of their children were rocks, some were eels, and others were sea creatures of various kinds. Two of their sons, Kumukahi and Palamoa, are believed by some to be identical to the same-named pair of Puna fame; others deny this.

Along the Wailuku River, in the area called Waimalino by Reeds Island, are two stone "brothers." What family they belong to is no longer known. The older brother is called Konanuhea and the younger is called Mu. They are said to have had two other brothers. One was a *kupua* (being with supernatural powers) who could take the form of an *'anuhe* (caterpillar) or a chief. When in the form of a chief, however, he retained a tail like a caterpillar. The other brother, whose name was Mano, is at Waianuenue or "Rainbow Falls." He too was a *kupua* and could take the form of either a turtle, *'aha* fish, or eel.

The most famous stone "family" in the area is that of Kana and Pohaku Hanau. Little is known of the mother or her background—even her true name remains unknown. Today she is called Pohaku Hanau or "Reproducing Stone." She may be found at Kuipaa in the

Kapehu branch of the Wailuku River. It is said that Kana, the father, was not always a rock; he was born as a rope that could stretch. His unusual ability to stretch great distances led to many adventures and the stories of his exploits are used to explain many strange markings or rock outcrops found on all the Hawaiian islands.

One of Kana's most famous adventures occurred when his mother, Hina, was kidnapped from Hilo by a Molokai chief, who carried her away on the back of a turtle. With a brother, Kana tried to rescue Hina but lost a fight with her guards. Next, he challenged the turtle to a stretching contest. When Kana lost that contest his grandmother was brought to Molokai to help him in more stretching contests. First she turned him into a rope, then a *pōhuehue* (morning glory vine), then a banana, and finally a spider so large that it stretched from Molokai to Hilo. While he was stretched out as a spider, Kana's brother grabbed Hina and rushed her back to Hilo.

Tradition does not say why or when Kana was turned into a rock or whether his children were born as rocks. His stone body can be found in the Wailuku River in the main gulch between Pukao Maui and Kapaukea.

Several other stones also carry Kana's name. It is believed that one son of Pohaku Hanau and Kana is an unpretentious rock where the Hilo breakwater runs out. His name is Keahua, which is also the name of the surf in that area.

Several other children of this family are said to be found along the Hilo waterfront. Pohaku o 'Alo is a long stone submerged in the sea at the boundary of Piopio and Kuuau Elua and in front of Waiolama. A son, Paikaka, is nearby. On the Hamakua side, in the breakers of Kawili, is Kupehau, a large stone that is not deeply submerged. When a swimmer dives down, he can feel cold water coming up, possibly from a spring.

In the other direction, on the Hamakua side of the Wailuku River, in the sea a little offshore near the Hilo side of Pukihae Stream, is the stone child Kauea. A healing stone, its name means "Breath-of-life." At the direction of a medical *kahuna,* the sick swam around the stone as part of a healing ceremony.

Kana was turned into a spider so large it stretched from Molokai to Hilo. (Ken Coffey)

Pohaku o 'Iwa is still another stone child. It can be found in a whirl-pool-like place where the Honolii breakers come in. It was said that when sand piled up near this rock a chief would die. In the same area is a rock that, according to tradition, flew over from Kauai, but it was not of this family.

Coming back toward Hilo is the bluff Malani, where there was once a *pu'uhonua* (place of refuge). In the sea opposite the ancient *heiau* site and at the end of the bluff in about two fathoms of water is a rock son, Kunui. A brother, Kuliilii, lies in shallow water near the shore between Kanoa and the mouth of Pukihae Stream. Some say that in reality Ku, not Kana, was the father of these two sons of Pohaku Hanau.

Along the shore on the Puueo side of the Wailuku River mouth, be-low the old railroad bridge, is a daughter, Puao, and a son, Haakua. A nearby sister was lost when the bridge was built. Named Ohuwai, she was believed to care for the aborted material from miscarriages until that material matured and swam away as sharks. Pieces of umbilical cord were also left in her care.

On the upper side of the main bridge over the Wailuku River is a stone brother named Ahuawa. It was believed that he made the waves of the harbor swell. When standing by that rock looking upstream on the left bank of the river, the stone Kawaakauhia Maui, "The-ahi-fishing-canoe of Maui," can be seen. According to tradition, it was once the canoe of the demigod Maui before it was turned into stone. Maui used it when he went to the island of that name and snared the sun over the mountain now called Haleakala.

On the end of the stone canoe is a path of grass called Namauu Paao. It is believed to have been planted by the high priest Paao, who came to Hawaii from Upolu, Samoa, around the eleventh or twelfth century. Finding Hawaii without a ruler, Paao returned to Samoa and brought back with him a chief named Pili from whom the Kamehameha dynasty descended. Some have said that if the river water rose until it nearly reached the grass on the stone, "its height was not worth mentioning, but if the water covered the grass, then indeed there was a high water, *wai nui*." Others say such a high water foretold a royal death or the overthrow of a ruler.

The last two stone sons born to Kana and Pohaku Hanau lie just above Death Falls. They are Huakuaikai and Huakuaiuka. They divide the river water that flows to the two falls. There are some who say that there is still another son further up the river beyond Puu 'O'o Ranch. His name is Papakolea.

The landmarks in this story were recorded by Theodore Kelsey in 1919 when he gathered this material. These are only some of the stone names and stories he found for this area. Unfortunately, even at that time their complete stories had been lost.

Kelsey's informants for these stories were Mrs. Daniel Porter (commonly called Kukona), Mrs. Ku'ihelani Ka'aumoana of Amau'ula, James Iokepa, Ben Brown, Naluahine Ka'opua, Mr. and Mrs. Kenoi, Mrs. Pahau, Mr. Paalani of Malanai, Lameka Ahulau, Moku Ahulau, Maia Ahulau, Luukapu, and Kinikini.

10
The Wizard Stones of Waikiki

On Kuhio Beach at Waikiki are four famous stones named Kapaemahu, Kahaloa, Kapuni, and Kinohi. According to tradition, they contain the spirits of four great "wizards," who arrived in Hawaii before the time of the great sixteenth-century chief Kakuihewa, ruler of Oahu. They are said to have come from Moaulanuiakea, Tahiti, where they were favorites of the chiefs.

Although tall and manly in stature and general bearing, older Hawaiians say they were feminine in their habits. Some have called them "unsexed," others say they were *mahu*. According to recent stories, Kapaemahu was a male healer; Kahaloa, a beneficent female; Kapuni, another male; and Kinohi, a female bringing blessings to homes.

Old stories say that upon their arrival in Hawaii the four visited Waikiki and then made a long tour of all the Hawaiian islands. In time they returned to Waikiki where they settled at a spot called Ulukou, not far from the site of today's Moana and Surfrider hotels.

The low, soft speech of the four Tahitians endeared them to the Hawaiians, who came to visit in great numbers. Among the visitors some were ill. The wizards cured them by the laying on of hands. Because of these healings and other wise acts, the fame of the four grew throughout Hawaii.

Tradition does not tell why the wizards came to Hawaii or why, in time, they left. But before their departure they asked the people to erect a permanent reminder of their visit and the many cures they had effected. The people chose four large rocks as a monument. The rocks were taken from the vicinity of the "bell rock" in Kaimuki. Two of the rocks were to be placed on the grounds of the wizards' Waikiki home and two at their usual bathing place in the sea.

On the night of Kane, the twenty-seventh night of the moon-month, thousands of Hawaiians, under the direction of the four wizards, began to move the rocks. The people worked until the stones were placed as directed. It is also said that idols indicating the hermaphrodite sex of the wizards were placed under each stone.

Today the wizard stones sit on Kuhio Beach. (Chris Kelley)

Then Kapaemahu, apparently the chief or leader of the four, named the largest stone for himself and gave powers to the stone. One by one the other three wizards did the same. The rituals, prayers, and celebration that followed lasted through another cycle of the moon. Then the four disappeared, never to be heard from again. All of this took place during "the periods of Maweke and Mulielialii." Tradition has it that the stones were placed on the shore directly opposite a spot in the outer reef known as the "Cave of the Shark God." Reportedly, those frequenting the sea in that area avoided the cave, keeping their eyes upon the shore and made a detour when they appeared to be coming in line with the rocks.

According to Queen Liliuokalani, Kapuni was "a rock or coral in the sea of peculiar shape that was noted for the waves breaking over it . . . and the chiefs delighted to stand on its waves or the *nalu* of Kapuni. . . . Not only the chiefs indulged in this sport but the kaukau *aliis* or *kukaepopolos* and the *lopas* joined."

"Kamehameha sought this place after the celebrated battle at Nuuanu. . . . It was during his residence here that Kaahumanu moved away from the party with her ladies and *kahus* and made her residence just where Governor Cleghorn's houses are. . . . Kaahumanu was quite pleased with the situation and from there went down to meet Kamehameha and his party and all joined in the pleasure of surf riding." It was near here that a young chief by the name of Kanihonui was killed for having an affair with Kaahumanu.

James H. Boyd, a cousin of the Cleghorns, said the rocks were "rediscovered" shortly after the turn of this century. Other stories relate how Princess Likelike, sister of King Kalakaua and Queen Liliuokalani, wife of Governor A. S. Cleghorn, and mother of Princess Kaiulani, always placed a lei on each stone when entering or leaving the water and offered a prayer. She died in 1887.

According to Boyd, it was around 1907 that Governor Cleghorn had the rocks exhumed from their bed of sand and placed "in position" in the same locality. His son, Princess Kaiulani's brother, Thomas Alexander Cleghorn, remembered, "My father built a two-story dwelling and had the Wizard Stones on our property facing Kalakaua. . . . As a child I played on and around the stones, knowing they held some strange and exciting *mana*—always respecting the lore connected with them."

When Governor Cleghorn wrote his will in 1910, item 20 said, "It is my wish and I hereby direct that the historical stones now upon the premises last above mentioned shall not be defaced or removed from said premises."

Sometime after Cleghorn's death the stones were offered to the Bishop Museum, which refused them. Later, in 1941, when the Cleghorn property was leased for a bowling alley, the stones were broken into several pieces during the excavation, probably to facilitate construction. In 1958 the area was taken over by the City and County of Honolulu for a park. When demolition of the old Waikiki Bowl began, the large stone of Kapaemahu was found. As demolition and clearing of the area continued, the other three wizard stones were found.

Because of their historical interest, the Parks Board decided to keep the stones in the area. In 1963, "so as not to mar the landscape or interfere with the use of the beach,'' the stones were deeply imbedded in the sand.

Early in 1980 the stones were again moved, and so-called "traditionalists," mostly non-Hawaiians unaware of the stones' history of moves along Waikiki Beach, received extensive if short-lived newspaper and television coverage protesting the move. After several months "in storage" while beach improvements were being made, the stones were moved to a location some fifty feet "up" the beach from their last site near the Moana and Surfrider hotels. There, with both Hawaiian and Christian blessings, the stones were placed under a banyon tree along Kalakaua Avenue.

Material for this story comes from the papers of Queen Liliuokalani in the Hawaii State Archives; an interview with Mrs. T. A. K. Cleghorn; personal correspondence with Mr. T. A. K. Cleghorn; the 1910 will of Governor A. S. Cleghorn and the probate records of his estate; an article in the 1907 *Hawaiian Annual* by James H. Boyd; notes of A. P. Taylor, former Territorial Archivist; notes of Mary Kawena Pukui; and various news stories reported over the years in the *Honolulu Advertiser* and *Honolulu Star-Bulletin*.